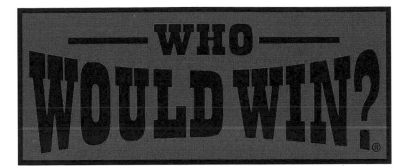

EXTREME
ANIMAL
RUMBLE

WHO WOULD WIN?

EXTREME ANIMAL RUMBLE

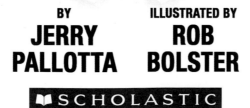

BY
JERRY PALLOTTA

ILLUSTRATED BY
ROB BOLSTER

SCHOLASTIC

The publisher would like to thank the following for their kind permission to use their photographs in this book: Photos ©: 103 top left: Martin M. Bruce/Superstock, Inc.; 103 bottom left: Volodymyr Burdiak/Shutterstock; 105 bottom: GOLFX/Shutterstock; 106 center: Martin M. Bruce/Superstock, Inc.; 115 to: Patrick K. Campbell/Shutterstock; 115 bottom: Curioso/Shutterstock; 117 top: lightstock/Thinkstock; 121 top: dangdumrong/Thinkstock; 125 bottom: Laura Ekleberry/Thinkstock; 127 top: Volodymyr Burdiak/Shutterstock.

Thank you #21, Malcolm Butler of the University of West Alabama.
Thank you for the lift --Sheila, Jill, Nancy, Janet, Ellen,
Jane, Christine, Eileen, and Liz.
Thank you to my favorite dinosaurs: Dan, Jay, Bergie, George,
Freddie, and Soupy.
Written especially for Hugh M. Dellelo.
To Andy Pallotta, the great white shark, and Kathy Pallotta,
the cookie-cutter shark.
—J.P.

To my friend Santiago of Westwood. The old man and the sea.
To David.
Thanks to the paleontologists who pieced together these amazing creatures.
Illustrated especially for baby Breslin.
To my brother Ed Griffin, for his generosity and biting wit.
⁻R.B.

ISBN 978-1-338-74530-6

10 9 8 7 6 5 4 3 2   21 22 23 24 25

Printed in China   62
This edition first printing, 2021

TABLE of CONTENTS

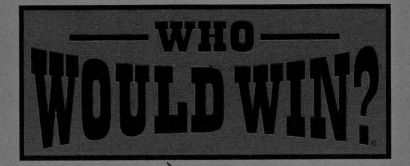

ULTIMATE
OCEAN
RUMBLE

16-CREATURE BRACKET

round 1

walrus
sand tiger shark

narwhal
torpedo fish

killer whale
sea snake

man o' war
leatherback turtle

polar bear
stonefish

saltwater crocodile
giant squid

great white shark
giant manta ray

sailfish
blue-ringed octopus

round 2

winner

winner

winner

winner

winner

winner

winner

winner

round 3

winner

winner

winner

winner

championship

winner

winner

**Ultimate
Ocean
Rumble
champion**

Sixteen sea creatures have agreed to participate in a bracketed battle. The first round has eight matches. It's single elimination. If a creature loses, it is out of the competition. Our first match is walrus versus sand tiger shark.

ROUND 1

WALRUS VS. SAND TIGER SHARK

MATCH 1

As soon as the walrus gets off the ice, it will face the hungry shark.

SAND TIGER WINS!

The walrus jumps off the ice floe and tries to outswi[m] sand tiger. The shark catches up and bites a flipper.

DID YOU KNOW?
Walrus skin is 3 to 4 inches thick.

The walrus is badly hurt. Its blubber didn't protect it. The sand tiger shark wins.

The second match in round one features a narwhal versus a torpedo fish. Who would win if they had a fight?

FACT
The long tusk of the narwhal is actually an overgrown tooth.

DID YOU KNOW?
A narwhal is an Arctic sea mammal that breathes air.

ROUND 1

NARWHAL VS. TORPEDO FISH

MATCH 2

The torpedo fish, also known as an electric ray, leaves the ocean bottom and swims toward the narwhal.

FACT
Most rays live close to the ocean floor.

SHOCKING FACT
The jolt of electricity from a torpedo fish is strong enough to kill a person.

NARWHAL WINS!

The torpedo fish attempts to give an electric shock to the narwhal. The intelligent narwhal scores a direct hit with its long, pointy tusk. Narwhal wins!

FACT

ELECTRIC FACT
After giving a shock, the torpedo fish has to "recharge itself" to give another shock.

The narwhal will now move on to round two and come face-to-face with the sand tiger shark.

The third match has a killer whale against a sea snake. The orca wants nothing to do with snakes. Snakes? Yuck!

DID YOU KNOW?
A killer whale is also known as an orca.

WILD FACT
Killer whales are always black and white. Most live in a group called a pod.

FACT
A killer whale that does not belong to a pod is called a rogue.

ROUND 1 — KILLER WHALE VS. SEA SNAKE — MATCH 3

It doesn't look like a fair fight. A giant sea mammal versus a skinny little reptile. Watch out, killer whale— a deadly, poisonous snake!

DEFINITION
Sea snakes have a tail shaped like an oar.

FUN FACT
Sea snakes look like eels, but they are not fish. They are reptiles.

KILLER WHALE WINS!

*Wham! The killer whale doesn't back down!
It blows bubbles and makes the sea snake dizzy.*

FACT
*A sea snake can hold its
breath for five hours.*

DID YOU KNOW?
*Orcas are considered
the greatest predators
on Earth.*

The killer whale pins the snake and breaks its bones.
The snake never saw it coming. The killer whale will
be moving on to the next round.

Our fourth match in round one has a Portuguese man o' war facing off against a leatherback turtle.

FACT
A man o' war is not a jellyfish.

IT'S TRUE
A man o' war is a siphonophore. That means it is actually made up of hundreds of smaller sea creatures.

FUN FACT
The tentacles of a man o' war can reach more than 100 feet long.

ROUND 1

MAN O' WAR VS. LEATHERBACK TURTLE

MATCH 4

This match showcases an excellent swimmer versus a drifter. The leatherback turtle's legs are like wings.

TWO FUN FACTS
Turtles are reptiles.
Turtles do not have teeth.

MAN O' WAR WINS!

The leatherback turtle is careless and swims into the stinging tentacles of the man o' war. The stinging poison gets in its eyes, nose, and throat. It proves to be deadly.

DRIFTING FACT
The man o' war drifts with wind, waves, currents, and tides.

BIG FACT
The leatherback turtle is the largest of all turtles. They can grow up to 7 feet long and weigh up to 2,000 pounds.

SWIM FACT
Leatherbacks are fast swimmers and can be found in all oceans.

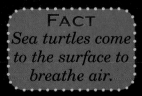

FACT
Sea turtles come to the surface to breathe air.

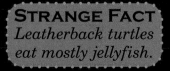

STRANGE FACT
Leatherback turtles eat mostly jellyfish.

Sorry, turtle! The man o' war wins the match.

What is a polar bear doing in an ocean book? Polar bears are considered sea mammals. They live on the Arctic Ocean's ice.

POLAR BEAR VS. STONEFISH

ROUND **1**

MATCH **5**

At the shoreline, the polar bear takes a walk into the ocean. The bear doesn't know there is a stonefish patiently waiting for a fish dinner to swim by.

STONEFISH WINS!

The stonefish is camouflaged and looks like rocks on the bottom. Oops! The polar bear steps on the stonefish. Ouch! The stonefish's deadly poison will kill the polar bear.

GROSS FACT
Stonefish poison is a neurotoxin. It makes your muscles stop moving, and you can't breathe.

STRONG FACT
Polar bears are so strong they can drag a 2,000-pound dead walrus with their teeth.

DID YOU KNOW?
Polar bears are excellent swimmers. People have witnessed them swim more than 50 miles.

The ugly stonefish will move on to the second round, but who will it fight?

The next match is the one everyone has been waiting for. It's still the first round, match number six! Saltwater crocodile versus giant squid.

NAME FACT
Sometimes saltwater crocodiles are nicknamed "Saltie."

FUN FACT
Saltie prefers to live in swamps, estuaries, and lagoons, but often swims in open ocean.

FACT
A saltwater crocodile is the largest reptile in the world. Yikes! They can measure 20 feet long.

ROUND 1 · SALTWATER CROCODILE VS. GIANT SQUID · MATCH 6

The saltwater crocodile is an ambush predator. It patiently waits for the giant squid to swim nearby. The squid is looking for something to eat.

FUN FACT
The giant squid has eight legs and two feeder arms. The underside of its legs are covered with suction cups.

SIZE FACT
A colossal squid is the widest squid. A giant squid is the longest squid.

SALTWATER CROCODILE WINS!

The saltwater crocodile flaps its huge tail and attacks in a burst of energy. It grabs the squid and takes a huge bite. The giant squid shoots ink, but Saltie doesn't even notice.

> ## ATTENTION!
> *An adult saltwater crocodile will eat any large animal, including humans!*

The saltwater crocodile wins. It is off to the second round.

Finally! The world-famous great white shark has entered the tournament. It's match number seven! Great white shark versus giant manta ray.

GREAT WHITE SHARK VS. GIANT MANTA RAY

ROUND 1

MATCH 7

This fight is teeth, teeth, and more teeth versus a filter feeder. The giant manta ray is huge. Maybe it can smack the shark silly.

DID YOU KNOW?
Manta ray wings can be as long as 30 feet from wing tip to wing tip. That's longer than most private airplanes.

DEFINITION
A filter feeder is an ocean creature that eats by straining small food from the water.

FACT
A giant manta ray can jump completely out of the ocean.

21

GREAT WHITE SHARK WINS!

The fearless shark goes right at the giant manta ray and bites it in the face. The great white enjoys the meal.

SIZE FACT
The largest of all rays is a giant manta ray. They can weigh up to 3,000 pounds! That's a ton and a half.

SHARP FACT
Great white shark teeth are serrated, triangular, and as sharp as steak knives.

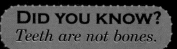

DID YOU KNOW?
Teeth are not bones.

The ferocious great white shark gets past round one. No one is surprised.

It's the last match of the first round. The sailfish meets up with a blue-ringed octopus.

FUN FACT
The large dorsal fin allows the sailfish to make sharp turns.

SPEED FACT
The sailfish is the fastest fish in the ocean. It can swim up to 90 miles per hour.

SAILFISH VS. BLUE-RINGED OCTOPUS

It's speed against poison! Fish versus mollusk!

POISON FACT
Many scientists say the blue-ringed octopus has the deadliest venom in all the oceans.

DEFINITION
Venom is liquid poison injected by an animal.

BLUE-RINGED OCTOPUS WINS!

The sailfish leaves deep water and swims near the coral reef, looking for food. The blue-ringed octopus gets startled and jumps on the sailfish's back.

DID YOU KNOW?
A sailfish is a pelagic fish.

DEFINITION
A pelagic fish is not found in one place. It swims all over the world.

As the fish shifts into high gear, the octopus injects its venom. The sailfish is out of the tournament.

The first round is over. Do the math. The tournament began with sixteen creatures. Half are out, so divide sixteen by two. Only eight are left.

Ding! Ding! Ding! Round two has begun. Narwhal versus sand tiger shark.

DID YOU KNOW?
Narwhals live in the Arctic, not the Antarctic.

NARWHAL VS. SAND TIGER SHARK

A fish against a whale is a great matchup. The narwhal has to come up for air. The shark doesn't. Who has the advantage?

FACT
Rays and sharks have no bones. Their skeletons are made of cartilage.

YOU SHOULD KNOW
Cartilage is not bone. It is what your ears and nose are made of.

SAND TIGER SHARK WINS!

The narwhal and the sand tiger fight back and forth.

DID YOU KNOW?

DID YOU KNOW?
Sharks do not get cancer.

FUN FACT
Narwhals do not have a dorsal fin.

The long tusk prevents the narwhal from making fast turns. The narwhal is no match for the shark! The shark wins!

It's round two, match two. The killer whale swims over to meet up with the man o' war.

KILLER WHALE VS. MAN O' WAR

ROUND **2**

MATCH **2**

Uh-oh! Is this a trick? Not one but hundreds of man o' wars are in the water.

MAN O' WAR WINS!

The killer whale accidentally sucks a man o' war into its blowhole. The poison and stinging tentacles enter the killer whale's lungs.

WARNING! POISON!
Never ever touch a man o' war. It has deadly chemicals that can hurt humans.

DID YOU KNOW?
A killer whale is the largest of all dolphins.

FUN FACT
A killer whale has no natural enemies and is not an endangered species.

The killer whale is in big trouble. Its mouth, tongue, sinuses, and lungs are burning from the deadly man o' war chemicals. It withdraws from the competition. Sadly, the much-anticipated match between the killer whale and the saltwater crocodile is not going to happen. There is always next year!

Round two, match three! This time it is saltwater crocodile versus stonefish. If this was a beauty contest, no one would want a photo taken with either creature.

ROUND 2 SALTWATER CROC. VS. STONEFISH MATCH 3

The crocodile uses its tail to muddy the water. Now the stonefish can't see well. Where is that crocodile?

SALTWATER CROC WINS!

The crocodile uses a smart tactic. While the stonefish is motionless on the bottom of the ocean, the crocodile uses its three-foot-long jaws to bite the stonefish sideways. Crunch! The spines never touch the crocodile.

DEFENSIVE FACT
A saltwater crocodile is so ferocious that even a small one is dangerous to humans.

FACT
Crocodiles often bury their prey underwater to eat later when the meat is more tender.

The reptile has won. The stonefish is dead. Saltwater crocodile is going to the semifinals!

This is the last match in round two. Great white shark versus blue-ringed octopus. Everyone expects the great white shark to advance to the finals.

GREAT WHITE SHARK VS. BLUE-RINGED OCTOPUS

ROUND **2**

MATCH **4**

Will the blue-ringed octopus become dinner for the most feared shark in the ocean? Is the blue-ringed octopus afraid? Is the great white shark smart enough to avoid the poison?

BLUE-RINGED OCTOPUS WINS!

The great white shark tries to swallow the blue-ringed octopus. But the shifty octopus doesn't get swallowed right away. It gets into the shark's gills.

One, two, three seconds, and the shark cannot shake the octopus. The octopus injects its deadly venom. The shark is losing consciousness. The great white shark stops swimming and sinks. It's not looking so "great."

The blue-ringed octopus moves on to the next round.

The second round is over. Should we call the next two matches the third round or the semifinals?

In basketball it's called the *Final Four*.
In ice hockey it's called the *Frozen Four*.
We now present the *Ocean Four*.

Wow! It's down to a siphonophore, a fish, a reptile, and a mollusk. The sea mammals can only watch.

MAN O' WAR VS. SAND TIGER SHARK

It's a sand tiger shark versus a man o' war. In baseball they might say "play ball!" We say, "May the best creature win!"

STRANGE FACT
The Ocean Four *are all cold-blooded animals.*

ANOTHER STRANGE FACT
Of the original sixteen sea creatures, the killer whale, walrus, narwhal, and polar bear are warm-blooded animals.

The sand tiger shark flicks its tail and breaks the man o' war into pieces. The shark gets stung, but it shakes it off. The shark has toothlike skin. The man o' war gets caught in a current and washes up on the beach.

TOOTH FACT
The hard, rough "teeth" on a shark's skin are called denticles.

The sun's heat kills the beached man o' war. Watch out! Even dead, it's still poisonous. Don't ever touch one. The sand tiger shark moves on to the finals.

And now the other half of the *Ocean Four*! Saltwater crocodile versus blue-ringed octopus. Saltie has defeated the giant squid and the stonefish.

SALTWATER CROC VS. BLUE-RINGED OCTOPUS

The octopus has already defeated the sailfish and the great white shark. Saltie is not fooling around. It heads straight for the blue-ringed octopus. Beware of its poison!

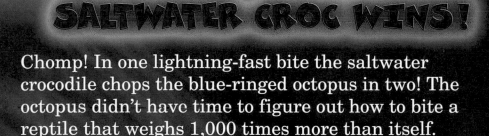

SALTWATER CROC WINS!

Chomp! In one lightning-fast bite the saltwater crocodile chops the blue-ringed octopus in two! The octopus didn't have time to figure out how to bite a reptile that weighs 1,000 times more than itself.

WEIGHT FACT
A saltwater crocodile can weigh up to 2,000 pounds. That's a ton!

WEIGHT FACT
A blue-ringed octopus weighs only two pounds.

DISTANCE FACT
Scientists tagged a saltie and recorded it swimming 600 miles in open ocean.

Poison is a great weapon, but this time it didn't help. The nasty saltwater crocodile is heading to the finals!

It's the final match of the tournament. Sand tiger shark versus saltwater crocodile. Can the rugged shark beat the nastiest reptile on Earth?

BEWARE!
Most shark attacks happen at dusk, in estuaries or in cloudy water.

CHAMPIONSHIP MATCH!

PAY ATTENTION!
Most saltwater crocodile attacks occur near the shoreline or in crocodile-infested lagoons.

The smaller sand tiger shark is too timid for the huge, ferocious saltwater crocodile.

SALTWATER CROC WINS!

The crocodile positions itself just right and delivers a fatal bite to the shark. It's over! The biggest, meanest reptile on Earth wins! The saltwater crocodile wins the Ultimate Ocean Rumble.

This is one way the competition might have ended. How would you rewrite the brackets?

WHO WOULD WIN?®

ULTIMATE BUG RUMBLE

16-CREATURE BRACKET

round 1

round 2

round 3

championship

black widow spider
dragonfly
winner

centipede
assassin bug
winner

winner

butterfly
killer bee
winner

praying mantis
cockroach
winner

winner

winner

hornet
tiger beetle
winner

daddy longlegs
scorpion
winner

winner

stinkbug
woolly bear
winner

cicada
tarantula
winner

winner

winner

Ultimate
Bug
Rumble
champion

No one knows why it happened, but sixteen bugs and insects just showed up for a bracketed contest. The rules are simple. If you lose, you are out of the tournament. Who will win?

LEG FACT
Insects have six legs. Spiders have eight.

ROUND 1

BLACK WIDOW SPIDER VS. DRAGONFLY

MATCH 1

The dragonfly is soaring around. It flies close to the web of a black widow spider.

FUN FACT
Dragonflies have four wings. They can fly forward and backward, and they can hover.

DID YOU KNOW?
There are thousands of different species of dragonflies.

BONUS FACT
A dragonfly has six legs but it can't walk.

BLACK WIDOW SPIDER WINS!

The tip of the dragonfly's wing gets caught in the web of the spider. The black widow has bad eyesight, but it feels the vibrations of the trapped dragonfly.

FUN FACT
Spiders are not insects. Spiders are arachnids.

IDENTI-FACT
Dragonflies are easy to recognize. They have long bodies and see-through wings.

As the dragonfly tries to free itself, the black widow attacks. The spider bites the dragonfly and injects it with deadly venom. The dragonfly will be dinner.

A centipede has no wings and cannot fly, but it is good at walking. The centipede sees an assassin bug. This could be trouble.

CENTIPEDE VS. ASSASSIN BUG

ROUND **1**

MATCH **2**

The centipede is scary looking. Will the assassin bug just run away? No! The assassin bug faces the oncoming centipede.

CENTIPEDE WINS!

At first, the assassin bug is aggressive. But the flexible centipede moves its body quickly and uses its multiple legs to pin the assassin bug.

DEFINITION
An assassin is someone who kills for money or fame.

FACT
The centipede has a pair of legs for each segment of its body.

One! Two! Three! The centipede bites a chunk out of the assassin bug. The centipede will go on to fight the black widow spider.

A butterfly? What are you doing in this competition? You should be in a beauty contest, not a fight.

BUTTERFLY VS. KILLER BEE

This unusual matchup has a colorful flier versus a dangerous stinging insect.

KILLER BEE WINS!

The butterfly flies around, trying to confuse the killer bee. The killer bee heads straight for the butterfly and stings it in the head. The butterfly stops flying and crashes. It dies.

FACT
A butterfly's best defense is to fly away.

STINGING FACT
A swarm of killer bees could kill almost any animal. People must avoid killer bees.

DEFINITION
A swarm is a dense group of flying insects.

Bees can sting a human only once. They can sting soft insects multiple times. The killer bee moves on to the second round.

The spiky front legs of a praying mantis are designed to catch prey. This insect normally eats whatever it can catch. The praying mantis turns its head and sees a cockroach.

BEHAVIOR FACT
A praying mantis is an ambush predator. It lies in wait to catch prey.

PRAYING MANTIS VS. COCKROACH

Watch out, praying mantis. The cockroach is a tough pest. It can live for weeks without food. Some can run up to three miles per hour. That's fast for an insect.

FACT
Cockroach antennae look like loose strings.

WING FACT
Cockroach wings overlap. Beetle wings fold neatly in a straight line.

cockroach   beetle

PRAYING MANTIS WINS!

This is not a quick fight. The praying mantis goes after the cockroach. The cockroach runs away. The praying mantis pursues and corners it.

FACT
Cockroaches are found from the Arctic to the tropics and in every type of environment.

DID YOU KNOW?
Some people keep praying mantises as pets.

The cockroach tries to fly, but the praying mantis hooks it with its front legs and damages it.

Crunch! Crunch! Bite! The praying mantis wins.

The next contest pairs a hornet with a tiger beetle. The hornet is hungry. It sees the tiger beetle.

ROUND 1

HORNET VS. TIGER BEETLE

MATCH 5

The tiger beetle prefers to walk, but it has wings and can fly. These two insects are on a collision course.

HORNET WINS!

The aggressive hornet flies right at the tiger beetle. The tiger beetle fights back. After one sting, the tiger beetle thinks it's best to fly away. Now both insects are airborne, flying in circles, trying to attack each other.

> ### FACT
> *A hornet is in the wasp family of insects.*

> ### VISION FACT
> *A tiger beetle cannot see while running.*

The hornet can maneuver better in the air. It stings the tiger beetle several times. It gets harder for the wounded beetle to fly. The hornet wins and flies on to the second round.

RUMBLE UPDATE: Five matches down, three to go.

The daddy longlegs enters the competition. It is tall and skinny. It may be wondering if entering this contest was a good idea.

BODY-TYPE FACT
Look! It only has one body part. The head, thorax, and abdomen are all one.

FUN FACT
The daddy longlegs has eight legs but it is not a spider. It is in an order called harvestmen.

ROUND 1

DADDY LONGLEGS VS. SCORPION

MATCH 6

A scorpion is loaded with weapons: pincers, a biting mouth, and a stinging tail.

DID YOU KNOW?
A false scorpion looks identical to a scorpion, but it has no stinger.

SCORPION WINS!

The daddy longlegs ignores the scorpion and walks right over it. The daddy longlegs is so light, the scorpion hardly feels it.

The battle begins. The scorpion has too much firepower. Sting! Pinch! Sting! Pinch! The stinging scorpion wins! Aren't we humans lucky a scorpion isn't as big as a pickup truck?

If you touch or squeeze a stinkbug, it stinks. However, some people don't mind how these bugs smell.

YUMMY FACT
Some people eat stinkbugs. They say the bugs taste like apples. Yum!

ROUND 1 — STINKBUG VS. WOOLLY BEAR — MATCH 7

Should a gentle caterpillar be in this book? Oh well! The fight is on.

FACT
A caterpillar is the larva of a butterfly or a moth. This woolly bear is a tiger moth.

DEFINITION
The larval stage is the immature stage of an insect's life.

FACT
Some woolly bears are blond.

WOOLLY BEAR WINS!

The woolly bear coughs up some slime, which smells awful. Even the stinkbug doesn't like it. The two bugs meet! The woolly bear refuses to fight and rolls itself into a ball.

> **FACT**
> *Stinkbugs are in a class of insects known as "true bugs."*

Suddenly a bird swoops in and eats the stinkbug. The woolly bear caterpillar wins by accident, which sometimes happens in the animal kingdom.

The crowd is chanting! "Fuzzy! Fuzzy! Fuzzy!" It sounds like the fuzzy woolly bear may be a fan favorite!

Our last match of the first round is a noisy cicada versus a big hairy spider. Welcome the tarantula, our sixteenth contestant.

SHEDDING FACT
Both of these creatures shed their skin, which is called molting.

STRANGE FACT
Some cicadas come out of the ground only once, after seventeen years, then die five to six weeks later.

ROUND **1**

CICADA VS. TARANTULA

MATCH **8**

FACT
The tarantula has eight legs. The two long appendages next to its mouth are called palps.

OLD-AGE FACT
Some tarantulas live up to thirty years. Cicadas live for less than six weeks.

The tarantula gets annoyed listening to the cicada, the loudest insect in the world.

TARANTULA WINS!

This is a mismatch. Wham! The heavy tarantula jumps on the cicada and sinks its fangs in. The cicada stops singing.

FACT
A cicada makes noise by vibrating its bumpy exoskeleton.

DEFINITION
Bugs do not have bones. They have an exoskeleton, which is an exterior shell.

On to the second round!

Welcome to round two. We have the black widow spider fighting the centipede. Insects have six legs, so neither of these bugs is an insect.

ROUND (2) BLACK WIDOW SPIDER VS. CENTIPEDE MATCH 1

The centipede may be the most surprising of all the contestants. No one expected it to get this far.

CENTIPEDE WINS!

The centipede is overpowering. The black widow spider tries to bite, but its tender body can't handle the weight and shiftiness of all those centipede legs.

DANGER!

If you get bitten by a black widow, go to the hospital right away.

NUMBER FACT

The black widow is on top, then the centipede is on top. The fight goes back and forth.

Bite! The centipede wins. Sorry, black widow. You lost.

The killer bee returns for round two. It has a nasty look. Other bugs should beware! It will fight the praying mantis. The fans can't wait!

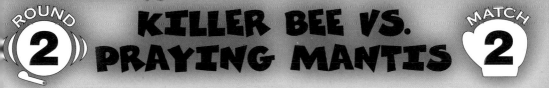

ROUND 2 KILLER BEE VS. PRAYING MANTIS MATCH 2

The praying mantis has quick reflexes. The killer bee is a better flier. Usually only male praying mantises can fly.

PRAYING MANTIS WINS!

The killer bee tries to sting the praying mantis. But the praying mantis is too quick. Its strong arms grab the killer bee out of the air. The bee tries a spin-and-sting move.

KNEELING FACT
The praying mantis got its name because its front legs make it look like it is kneeling in worship.

The praying mantis bites first, which ends the fight quickly. The praying mantis moves on to the next round. The killer bee did not live up to its name.

This match is bad attitude versus more bad attitude. Flying stinger versus stinger and pincers. Six legs versus eight legs.

DID YOU KNOW?
The biggest hornet in the world is the Asian giant hornet.

ROUND
2

HORNET VS. SCORPION

MATCH
3

FACT
One of the deadliest scorpions is known as a deathstalker.

This matchup is everything an Ultimate Bug Rumble fan could want.

HORNET WINS!

The hornet avoids the scorpion's strength by attacking from above. Seeing an opening, the hornet stings the scorpion and flies away. Ouch! It sees another opportunity and stings again. Ouch!

POISON FACT
Both hornets and scorpions have venom in their stingers.

SHARP FACT
Hornets and scorpions can sting multiple times.

A couple more stings, and the scorpion is badly hurt. It loses strength. The hornet's strategy works. Scorpions can't fly, so airpower wins!

Fuzzy! Fuzzy! Fuzzy! This fan favorite is back for round two. It's fuzzy versus hairy.

ROUND

2

WOOLLY BEAR VS. TARANTULA

MATCH

4

It looks like the tarantula will have an easy opponent.

TARANTULA WINS!

The woolly bear rolls itself into a ball. The tarantula is not fooled.

NICKNAME

The woolly bear is also called the black-ended bear or the woolly worm.

The tarantula pounces on the woolly bear. The tarantula sinks its fangs in. Fuzzy lost.

Round two is over. Centipede, praying mantis, hornet, and tarantula are heading to the semifinal round, which we'll call the "Bug Four"!

The second round is over. Welcome to the third round, or Bug Four. It has been an exciting single-elimination fight. Get ready for the multilegged centipede to fight the bug-eating praying mantis.

50/50 FACT
Half of the Bug Four are insects.

CENTIPEDE VS. PRAYING MANTIS

The fans will be watching all of those legs. The praying mantis has six. It looks like the centipede has a million.

OCEAN FACT
A mantis shrimp has the same snatching arms as a praying mantis.

The centipede crawls over the praying mantis. It tries to bite but the praying mantis flies away. Every time the centipede gets close, the praying mantis seems to escape.

EXPENSIVE FACT

Aren't you glad you don't have to buy shoes for the centipede?

The praying mantis bites one leg off the centipede, then another. After removing a few more legs, the praying mantis delivers a fatal bite. Praying mantis, you are going to the finals!

It's the hornet versus the tarantula. This fight may not be fair. The hornet has already defeated the tiger beetle and the scorpion.

ROUND 3 **HORNET VS. TARANTULA** **MATCH 2**

The tarantula has big fangs, but it has no wings. The tarantula has defeated the cicada and the woolly bear. Who will get to the finals?

HORNET WINS!

The hornet wastes no time. It buzzes toward the tarantula's face. The tarantula gets up on its hind legs and tries boxing. It misses. The hornet flies in circles and does a loop-the-loop. The hornet then stings the tarantula.

The hornet keeps stinging it. It stings so many times, the tarantula stops walking and collapses. The hornet flies on to the final match.

CHAMPIONSHIP MATCH!

It's the final fight of the tournament: praying mantis versus hornet. The praying mantis flies, then tries to snatch and bite off the hornet's head. The hornet buzzes away.

The fight goes airborne! The heavily armed hornet is too quick. It stings the praying mantis multiple times. These two insects fight back and forth. The mantis is usually a great fighter, but the smaller, faster hornet is more aggressive.

HORNET WINS!

Just as the praying mantis thinks it has the hornet in its grasp, the hornet outmaneuvers the praying mantis. With a sting, sting, sting, the praying mantis falls over. Too much firepower. The hornet wins!

This is one way the competition might have ended. Write your own ending or think of a new version of an Ultimate Rumble book.

WHO WOULD WIN?®

ULTIMATE DINOSAUR RUMBLE

16-DINOSAUR BRACKET

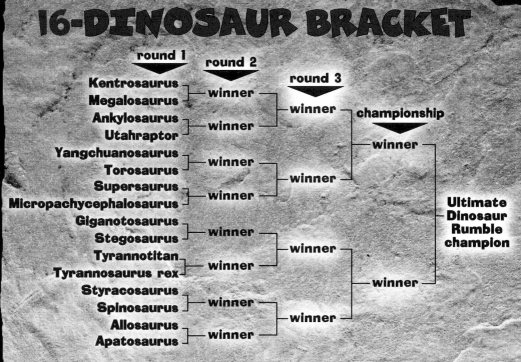

round 1

round 2

Kentrosaurus
Megalosaurus
— winner —

Ankylosaurus
Utahraptor
— winner —

round 3

— winner —

championship

— winner —

Yangchuanosaurus
Torosaurus
— winner —

Supersaurus
Micropachycephalosaurus
— winner —

— winner —

Ultimate
Dinosaur
Rumble
champion

Giganotosaurus
Stegosaurus
— winner —

Tyrannotitan
Tyrannosaurus rex
— winner —

— winner —

— winner —

Styracosaurus
Spinosaurus
— winner —

Allosaurus
Apatosaurus
— winner —

— winner —

Sixteen dinosaurs showed up for a contest to see who is the roughest and toughest. If a dinosaur loses a fight, it is out of the contest. May the most ferocious dinosaur win!

No pterosaurs allowed!

No plesiosaurs allowed!

"I'm a flying reptile."

"I'm an ocean-going reptile."

DID YOU KNOW?
The word dinosaur means "terrible lizard."

The first match is Kentrosaurus versus Megalosaurus. Kentrosaurus would not be easy to attack or eat. It is spiky.

ROUND 1 KENTROSAURUS VS. MEGALOSAURUS MATCH 1

NAME FACT
Megalosaurus means "big lizard."

Megalosaurus was the first dinosaur to be discovered and named. Its fossilized bones were dug up in England.

Megalosaurus attacks with its toothy jaw but Kentrosaurus is too spiky, pointy, and bumpy.

NAME FACT
Kentrosaurus means "prickly lizard."

Megalosaurus puts up a good fight but it's out of the competition.

KENTROSAURUS WINS!

Ankylosaurus had a large, solid bump on the end of its tail. Its skin was heavily armored.

ROUND 1

ANKYLOSAURUS VS. UTAHRAPTOR

MATCH 2

Utahraptor stars in the film *Jurassic World*. This movie-star dinosaur was about 23 feet long, but only eight feet tall. That is about as tall as two first graders.

Is this a fair fight? Ankylosaurus is covered in armor.

Utahraptor tries to sneak up on Ankylosaurus and slice its unprotected belly. But *whoosh!* One swipe from Ankylosaurus's tail and Utahraptor is knocked silly. Ankylosaurus moves on to the second round.

ANKYLOSAURUS WINS!

DID YOU KNOW?
Paleontologists now think the Utahraptor had feathers.

Yangchuanosaurus was discovered in China. When its remains were first discovered, people thought they were real dragon bones. Some people in other places also once believed this. Yangchuanosaurus was bipedal.

DEFINITION
Bipedal means an animal that walks on two legs.

YANGCHUANOSAURUS VS. TOROSAURUS

Torosaurus had the largest skull of any animal that ever lived on land. Its skull was as big as an elephant.

NAME FACT
Torosaurus means "perforated lizard."

DEFINITION
Perforated means "having holes." Torosaurus had holes in its shield-like skull.

FRILL FACT
The back of Torosaurus's skull is called its frill.

After dodging Torosaurus's sharp horns, Yangchuanosaurus bites its legs and slows down Torosaurus. The limping Torosaurus is done for. In this fight, the meat-eater defeats the plant-eater. The biped beats the quadruped.

NAME FACT
This dinosaur's name means "lizard found in the town of Yangchuan."

DEFINITION
A quadruped is an animal that walks on four legs.

YANGCHUANOSAURUS WINS!

Not fair! Who matched these two together? Supersaurus is fighting Micropachycephalosaurus. Supersaurus was a giant plant-eating sauropod.

> ## DEFINITION
> *Sauropod dinosaurs had long necks, small brains, long tails, and walked on four thick legs.*

SUPERSAURUS VS. MICROPACHYCEPHALOSAURUS

Micropachycephalosaurus is one of the longest names of any dinosaur. It's a long name, but it was a tiny dinosaur. It was only as big as a goose. Its name means "small, thick-headed lizard."

> ## HEAD FACT
> *No one knows why the Micropachycephalosaurus had such a thick skull.*

79

Supersaurus steps on Micropachycephalosaurus.
Uh-oh! Squished!

SUPERSAURUS WINS!

BIG FACT
*Sauropods were the largest
land animals ever.*

Supersaurus moves to the second round.

Giganotosaurus had a huge jaw full of sharp teeth. Its jaw was six feet long. Giganotosaurus is considered the largest meat-eating dinosaur. You would not want to fight it. It walked and hunted on two legs.

WHAT'S IN A NAME?
Giganotosaurus means "giant lizard of the south."

DEFINITION
Two-legged dinosaurs are called theropods. Theropod means "beast foot." Theropods walked like birds.

GIGANOTOSAURUS VS. STEGOSAURUS

This dinosaur is easy to recognize. It had plates on its back and a spiked tail.

NAME FACT
Stegosaurus means "roof lizard."

MYSTERY
Did Stegosaurus have matching plates or alternating plates on its back?

It is no fun fighting Stegosaurus's plates and spiked tail, but Giganotosaurus's powerful jaw overpowers the slow Stegosaurus. After a vicious fight, Giganotosaurus wins.

GIGANOTOSAURUS WINS!

BRAIN FACT
Stegosaurus had the smallest brain-compared-to-body-size of any dinosaur. Its brain was only the size of a walnut.

DON'T BE CONFUSED
A different dinosaur had a similar name, Gigantosaurus. It was a sauropod.

Tyrannotitan lived about 100 million years ago. In real life it would never have met a Tyrannosaurus rex, or T. rex, which lived at a later time. Because Tyrannotitan lived in an earlier age, its brain was probably not as developed as T. rex's.

NAME FACT
Tyrannotitan means "giant tyrant."

TYRANNOTITAN VS. TYRANNOSAURUS REX

JUST CALL ME T. REX

Everyone knows this creature. It's one of the most famous dinosaurs. "Go, T. rex, go!"

TIMELINE
T. rex lived about 65 million years ago.

T. rex is smarter. It runs at Tyrannotitan and bites off an arm. Tyrannotitan is shocked.

As it decides what to do next, T. rex charges full speed and bites a chunk out of its neck. The fight is over!

T. REX WINS!

Horns, horns everywhere! It would hurt to bite this dinosaur's face. Styracosaurus was an herbivore. Its teeth were perfect for slicing and munching plants.

FACT
Little horns are called hornlets.

ROUND 1

STYRACOSAURUS VS. SPINOSAURUS

MATCH 7

"SPIKED LIZARD" VS. "SPINED LIZARD"

Behold Spinosaurus! It may have been the perfect fighting dinosaur. It was fast, strong, light, and long. It had huge teeth on its jaw, and it could swim.

COLOR FACT
No one really knows what color the dinosaurs were or if they were multicolored.

Many dinosaur fans are rooting for Spinosaurus to win the championship. Spinosaurus could hunt on land and in the water. Go, Spinosaurus, go!

Spinosaurus goes head-to-head with Styracosaurus. Ouch! Too many sharp horns! They hurt. Styracosaurus is too slow.

Shifty Spinosaurus sneaks around to the back of Styracosaurus. Spinosaurus bites Styracosaurus in the rear end. Styracosaurus is bleeding. This fight is over! No surprise here. Speed beats horns.

SPINOSAURUS WINS!

Many Allosaurus fossils have been discovered around the world. One dig site alone in Utah produced 60 different Allosaurus specimens. This dinosaur ate meat and walked on two legs. Its vertebrae bones were shaped differently than other dinosaurs. We may never know if it hunted in packs or alone.

DEFINITION
Vertebrae are an animal's backbones.

NAME FACT
Allosaurus means "different lizard."

ALLOSAURUS VS. APATOSAURUS

Apatosaurus was a long sauropod-type dinosaur with a tail like a bullwhip. When this huge creature walked, it must have sounded like thunder.

TRICKY NAME
Apatosaurus means "deceptive lizard." It is sometimes confused with Brontosaurus, which means "thunder lizard."

Allosaurus runs, opens its mouth, and jumps on Apatosaurus. Apatosaurus is huge, between 75-85 feet long. Apatosaurus can defend itself well. It waits for Allosaurus to make another charge. It turns its body, sets its four legs, and whips its tail. *Whack!*

The tail hits Allosaurus across the neck and knocks the wind out of it. Another tail shot! *Whoosh! Whack!* That tail is huge! Allosaurus's neck is broken.

APATOSAURUS WINS!

Apatosaurus is the victor despite its small head and small brain.

On we go to the second round! Only eight dinosaurs are left. Kentrosaurus was armored with sharp weapons. It looked like it could inflict pain if attacked. Kentrosaurus did not look cute and huggable at all.

NAME FACT
A scientist that studies fossils and prehistoric life is called a paleontologist.

ROUND 2 — MATCH 1
KENTROSAURUS VS. ANKYLOSAURUS

Ankylosaurus was defensively armored and plated for protection. Its body was low to the ground and difficult to attack. It looked like a tank. It even had horns covering its neck.

FACT
Ankylosaurus was twice as big as Kentrosaurus.

Both of these dinosaurs were herbivores. These two don't eat each other, so why would they fight? They might battle over territory, plants to eat, or water to drink.

The smaller Kentrosaurus hits Ankylosaurus with its tail. Its tail bounces off Ankylosaurus's armor. Ankylosaurus gets close, swings its hammer-like tail, and breaks Kentrosaurus's leg bones. *Whack! Whack!* Kentrosaurus falls over.

TIMELINE
In geological time, the Jurassic period began around 200 million years ago.

ANKYLOSAURUS WINS!

Ankylosaurus moves on to what we'll call the DINO FINAL FOUR.

This is a fight that fans have been waiting for. Giganotosaurus was bigger than T. rex. They both had a similar body design. Giganotosaurus had a huge jaw and strong legs.

FACT
Giganotosaurus had three fingers on each short arm.

GIGANOTOSAURUS VS. TYRANNOSAURUS REX

T. rex had an advantage. Its jaw was much more powerful. Maybe T. rex was like an orca, also called a killer whale — a perfect hunting machine.

FOOT FACT
T. rex had four toes, just like a chicken. Three in front, one in back.

Giganotosaurus walks over to T. rex. It's not used to fighting an equal. T. rex pretends to bite but swings its body and whips Giganotosaurus with its heavy tail. T. rex attacks and gives Giganotosaurus something it didn't expect — a hip-check! While Giganotosaurus is off balance, T. rex bites Giganotosaurus's neck. T. rex doesn't let go!

TYRANNOSAURUS REX WINS!

Once again we have a meat-eater against a plant-eater. We also could describe this fight as:

- carnivore vs. herbivore
- enormous mouth vs. small mouth
- two legs vs. four legs
- hunter vs. forager

DEFINITION
An animal forager searches for plants and other foods to eat.

DID YOU KNOW?
Yangchuanosaurus weighed about three tons.

ROUND 2

YANGCHUANOSAURUS VS. SUPERSAURUS

MATCH 3

Supersaurus was one of the largest animals that ever walked on land. It weighed up to 40 tons. Its tail was up to 40 feet long. Its neck was longer than its tail.

OTHER HUGE SAUROPODS
Ultrasaurus, Giganotosaurus, Brachiosaurus, Argentinosaurus, or Diplodocus could have been in this book. How could they fight an aggressive, sharp-toothed meat-eater? Their size and height were great advantages.

As Yangchuanosaurus leaps and tries to bite chunks out of its foe, Supersaurus just trots toward Yangchuanosaurus and gets ready to step on it. Forty tons is a lot of weight. Supersaurus's body is high in the air, hard for Yangchuanosaurus to reach. Supersaurus bumps the smaller dinosaur with its long neck, then rises up on its hind legs and crushes Yangchuanosaurus with its feet.

TIMELINE
The Triassic period began around 250 million years ago.

Yangchuanosaurus has broken ribs and a broken leg. Good-bye, Yangchuanosaurus!

SUPERSAURUS WINS!

Supersaurus is the third dinosaur to get to the DINO FINAL FOUR.

Apatosaurus was a huge dinosaur. It ate up to 800 pounds of vegetation per day. It was up to 75 feet long. Scientists say it kept on growing and growing.

APATOSAURUS VS. SPINOSAURUS

DID YOU KNOW?
Spinosaurus may have fought ancient crocodiles.

Spinosaurus can send shivers down your spine. It is fast, long, and has a strong jaw with scary teeth. It is bigger than a T. rex but first it must defeat Apatosaurus.

Spinosaurus walks near Apatosaurus but stays out of range of its swinging head and whiplike tail. When Apatosaurus turns its head, Spinosaurus jumps up and rips a chunk out of its shoulder. Apatosaurus's shoulder starts bleeding. Spinosaurus runs to the other side and bites again.

SPINOSAURUSUS WINS!

Championship match coming soon!

DINO FINAL FOUR

This rugged plant-eater can smell the T. rex. It knows the T. rex is a troublemaker.

ROUND 3 — ANKYLOSAURUS VS. TYRANNOSAURUS REX — MATCH 1

When it was younger, T. rex got whacked by an Ankylosaurus tail. It hasn't forgotten the painful bump it got on its head.

T. rex runs full speed with its head down. *Smash!* T. rex knows the Ankylosaurus's armor is too thick to bite. T. rex needs to flip it over so it can bite its softer belly. Ankylosaurus is now helpless on its back.

T. rex takes a giant bite and moves on to the championship match.

T. REX WINS!

It sounds like thunder as Supersaurus approaches Spinosaurus. *Boom! Boom! Boom!* go its feet.

SUPERSAURUS VS. SPINOSAURUS

> **QUESTION?**
> *Would the versatile Spinosaurus prefer to fight on land, in a swamp, or in deep water?*

> **DEFINITION**
> *Versatile means able to adapt to different situations.*

Spinosaurus is fast. It runs at Supersaurus and attacks it between its front and back legs.

Spinosaurus has plenty of energy. It bites and backs off, then bites and backs off again. Spinosaurus avoids Supersaurus's huge tail and long neck. It takes time, but Supersaurus loses too much blood and eventually collapses.

SPINOSAURUS WINS!

On to the finals!

CHAMPIONSHIP MATCH!
TYRANNOSAURUS REX VS. SPINOSAURUS

The long-necks are gone! The armored dinosaurs are gone! The plant-eaters are gone! The spiked dinosaurs are gone! The plated dinosaurs are gone!

This is the fight that readers and dinosaurs have been waiting for — Jaw vs. Jaw!

T. rex has a stronger and wider jaw. Spinosaurus is longer but thinner. Spinosaurus also has a longer jaw. Both dinosaurs have a mouth full of sharp teeth. T. rex charges, but quicker Spinosaurus jumps out of the way.

101

Spinosaurus runs headfirst and bites T. rex's jaw. Spinosaurus's biting muscles are way stronger than the muscles T. rex uses to open its mouth.

Spinosaurus bites harder and deeper. Now T. rex can't bite back. Spinosaurus holds on. It uses its longer arms to scratch T. rex. T. rex loses.

SPINOSAURUS WINS!

This is one way the competition might have ended. Write your own ending or think of a new version of an Ultimate Rumble book.

WHO WOULD WIN?

ULTIMATE JUNGLE RUMBLE

16-CREATURE BRACKET

round 1

round 2

round 3

championship

hyena
monitor lizard — winner
gorilla
black mamba — winner
capybara
poison dart frog — winner
peacock
bongo — winner
red panda
warthog — winner
green anaconda
mandrill — winner
leopard
okapi — winner
anteater
sun bear — winner

winner

winner

winner

winner

winner

winner

winner

Ultimate
Jungle
Rumble
champion

Sixteen jungle creatures gather for a bracketed competition. The rules are simple. If you lose your match, you are out of the contest. Who will win?

HYENA VS. MONITOR LIZARD

The hyena faces the monitor lizard. These two animals are ready to fight.

SIZE FACT

A monitor lizard can grow up to five feet long and stand on its hind legs. It is one of the largest lizards in the world.

DID YOU KNOW?

The Komodo dragon is the largest lizard on Earth.

This fight pits a reptile against a mammal. The monitor lizard is rugged and tough, but it may be no match for the hyena.

JAW FACT
A hyena has powerful jaws that can break bones.

HYENA WINS!

The hyena knocks the lizard over and bites a chunk out of it. The hyena wins.

Many gorillas have black fur. Gorillas are sociable, which means they live in families with other gorillas.

GORILLA VS. BLACK MAMBA

ROUND 1

MATCH 2

The black mamba is a fast, venomous snake. It is matched against a gorilla, the largest of all apes.

COMPARE
What's the difference between venomous and poisonous? When you bite or touch an animal and get sick, that animal is poisonous. When an animal bites, stings, or stabs you, injects venom, and makes you sick, that animal is venomous.

SPEED FACT
The black mamba can slither up to twelve miles per hour.

The intelligent gorilla knows the black mamba is dangerous. The snake aims to give a fatal bite.

GORILLA WINS!

The gorilla picks up a heavy rock and drops it on the snake. The gorilla defeats the snake!

COLOR FACT
The black mamba got its name because the skin color on the inside of its mouth is black.

A capybara is the largest of all rodents. Today it will fight a poison dart frog.

FEET FACT
Capybaras have webbed feet and are great swimmers.

CAPYBARA VS. POISON DART FROG

ROUND **1**

MATCH **3**

The frog is small, but watch out. It is poisonous! The poison dart frog is a bright color to warn other animals to stay away. Can it win this battle?

WARNING!
The skin of a poison dart frog is toxic. Don't touch it, don't eat it!

FACT
Frogs do not have claws or toenails.

The fight begins. The capybara is usually friendly with other animals. Today it has a problem. How can it win? Biting the poisonous frog would kill the capybara.

TINY FACT
Most poison dart frogs are the size of a golf ball or smaller.

CAPYBARA WINS!

The heavy capybara rolls over the frog, squishes it, and wins! The capybara's fur protects it from the frog's poisonous skin. It will move on to the second round.

A peacock in the contest? It is a show-off, not a fighter. The peacock has sharp claws. Will its colorful display of feathers help it or hinder it?

ROUND 1

PEACOCK VS. BONGO

MATCH 4

The peacock is matched against a bongo. A bongo is the largest antelope that lives in the jungle. It can weigh up to nine hundred pounds.

SMALL FACT
The smallest antelope is the royal antelope.

The peacock flashes its tail feathers. It stares down the bongo. The bongo is not impressed. The bongo lowers its horns and tramples the peacock.

BONGO WINS!

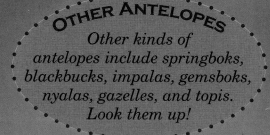

OTHER ANTELOPES

Other kinds of antelopes include springboks, blackbucks, impalas, gemsboks, nyalas, gazelles, and topis. Look them up!

The next matchup is a red panda against a warthog. The red panda is an herbivore, an animal that eats mostly plants. A red panda usually lives in a forest where bamboo grows.

BLANKET FACT
When cold, the red panda uses its fluffy tail as a blanket.

The red panda is the cutest animal in this book. It looks like a cross between a toy, a raccoon, and a house cat.

ROUND 1 **RED PANDA VS. WARTHOG** **MATCH 5**

SWINE FACT
Pigs, hogs, wild boars, and warthogs are all related. Oink!

DID YOU KNOW?
A baby warthog is called a piglet.

The warthog is an omnivore, an animal that eats everything.

The warthog and the red panda fight. The warthog has nasty teeth and is more aggressive than the red panda.

WARTHOG WINS!

Next is a snake against a monkey. The green anaconda is one of the largest snakes in the world. The mandrill has a colorful face. It looks like it is going to a Halloween party.

GREEN ANACONDA VS. MANDRILL

ROUND **1**

MATCH **6**

The mandrill is smart. It stares at the snake. The mandrill takes the situation seriously.

The fight begins. The mandrill hopes it is strong enough to bend the snake's neck. Unfortunately, it doesn't work. The snake is too tough.

CONSTRICTOR
The anaconda is a constrictor, which means it squeezes until its prey can't breathe.

DID YOU KNOW?
One mandrill alone in the wild is unusual. In real life, a horde of mandrills might chase a snake away.

GREEN ANACONDA WINS!

The snake grabs the mandrill. The snake's many muscles work together, squeezing tighter and tighter. The snake is heading to the second round.

The leopard is one of the greatest hunters in the animal kingdom. It is sneaky, strong, and has powerful jaws and deadly claws.

ROUND 1

LEOPARD VS. OKAPI

MATCH 7

An okapi looks like part giraffe and part horse. It is a plant eater, but it can defend itself by using its huge size and kick.

One good kick from the okapi could break the leopard's jaw. A broken jaw would doom the leopard.

The leopard sneaks up behind the okapi. The cunning leopard avoids getting kicked. It bites the okapi's hind leg. Ouch! Now the okapi has trouble walking.

SIZE FACT
A leopard can fight, kill, and eat an animal much larger than itself.

LEOPARD WINS!

The leopard jumps on the okapi's back and bites. The okapi is losing blood. Limping and bleeding, the okapi puts up a fight but eventually loses. The leopard moves on to the second round.

It's the last match of the first round. A giant anteater will fight a sun bear. The anteater eats insects. Its long sharp claws rip open ant mounds so the anteater can snag the ants with its long sticky tongue.

> **DEFINITION**
> *Animals that eat only bugs are called* insectivores.

ANTEATER VS. SUN BEAR

ROUND **1**

MATCH **8**

> **SOME KINDS OF BEARS**
> *Brown bear, black bear, polar bear, sun bear, grizzly bear, and spectacled bear.*

The anteater's long tongue will not help in fighting the sun bear.

The sun bear walks over to the anteater and slaps its banana-shaped head. The anteater tail is long and bushy, but it can't hurt the sun bear.

The bear attacks in force, punching, biting, and stomping on the anteater. The sun bear gets a minor scratch from the anteater's claws, but that's about it. The sun bear defeats the anteater.

SUN BEAR WINS!

The eight remaining contestants move on to the second round.

The hyena is ready to fight the gorilla. The gorilla has a weight advantage: about four hundred pounds vs. about two hundred pounds.

LAUGH
Hyena noises sound like laughing and giggling. This animal is sometimes called a laughing hyena.

HEAD FACT
A hyena has a large neck, head, and jaws for its size.

ROUND 2
HYENA VS. GORILLA
MATCH 1

FUN FACT
A gorilla's head is larger than a human's head, but a human's brain is bigger than a gorilla's brain.

DID YOU KNOW?
Gorillas can stand or walk on two legs.

The gorilla is the stronger animal.

The hyena tries to bite the gorilla. The gorilla outmaneuvers the hyena. Like a wrestler, the gorilla puts the hyena into a headlock.

AGE FACT
Gorillas live to be about 35–45 years old.

The hyena's scary jaws are not in position to bite the gorilla. The gorilla swings its body around and uses its weight to pounce on the hyena. The hyena is in trouble.

The gorilla moves on to what we'll call the Jungle Four.

The bongo is back after defeating the peacock. It must face the capybara, which defeated the poison dart frog.

HORN FACT

Bongo and rhinoceros horns are made of keratin, a protein that's an important part of hair and fingernails. Antlers are bone.

BONGO VS. CAPYBARA

The rodent must use its sharp front teeth to survive. Or it could jump in a river and out-swim the bongo. But there is no water around!

FACT

A rodent's front teeth continue to grow through its lifetime.

The bongo is thinking, "I could use my horns."

The bongo lowers its head near the ground and runs at the capybara. The capybara jumps out of the way. The bongo tries this tactic again and again. The bongo keeps on missing but the capybara is getting tired.

BONGO WINS!

Eventually the bongo hits the capybara and causes damage. That's it for the big rodent! It is defeated. The bongo moves on to the next round. These jungle animals are tough!

This match features a mammal against a reptile. Legs vs. no legs. Two animals have already won their way to the Jungle Four. Now the warthog faces the green anaconda.

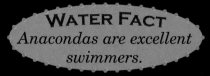

ROUND **2**

MATCH **3**

WARTHOG VS. GREEN ANACONDA

The warthog is faster, and the anaconda is stronger. The warthog has sharp teeth and tusks. The snake has small teeth but a strong squeeze. Does the snake want a ham sandwich? Maybe the warthog should just run away.

Trying to decide how to defeat the snake, the warthog wanders too close. The snake uses its teeth to grab its prey and wraps itself around the warthog. Uh-oh.

BODY FACT
A green anaconda can weigh more than five hundred pounds.

DINNER FACT
After eating the warthog, the snake won't have to eat again for months.

GREEN ANACONDA WINS!

The snake slowly tightens around the warthog. Eventually the boar can't breathe.

Not many people think of the sun bear as a ferocious animal. Its favorite foods are honey and insects. The leopard is known as an excellent hunter.

WEIRD COLOR FACT

Most black panthers are leopards or jaguars with no spots.

**ROUND 2**

LEOPARD VS SUN BEAR

MATCH 4

After this fight, the Jungle Four will be all set. So far we have a gorilla, bongo, and anaconda. Which animal will join them?

DID YOU KNOW?
The sun bear got its name from the marking on its chest.

The sun bear is strong and has sharp claws, but it is no match for the shifty cat. The leopard uses its paws to keep the bear off-balance.

LEOPARD WINS!

The leopard bites the bear. Repeated swipes and bites take their toll on the sun bear. The leopard moves to the third round!

THE JUNGLE FOUR

Round 3 has begun. Two African animals are in the same semifinal match. Fur against fur! The gorilla will fight the bongo.

DID YOU KNOW?
A gorilla does not have a tail.

 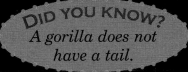 

ROUND 3

GORILLA VS. BONGO

MATCH 1

The two animals stare at each other. The bongo notices the gorilla's huge muscles. The gorilla sees the bongo's horns and large body.

NOWADAYS
A jungle is often called a rain forest.

This is an unusual fight. The bongo considers running away. It has no interest in the gorilla. The gorilla grabs and twists the bongo's hind leg. The gorilla is strong. It switches to the front of the bongo, grabbing its horns and twisting its front leg.

GORILLA WINS!

The bongo has trouble walking. The gorilla tips over the bongo, which crashes to the ground. The gorilla pins the bongo and wins. Who will the gorilla fight next?

Here's a fight that fans have been waiting for. Reptile against mammal! The anaconda from South America versus the leopard from Africa or Asia.

ROUND 3 GREEN ANACONDA VS. LEOPARD MATCH 2

The anaconda is not poisonous or venomous. The snake can't wait to wrap itself around this big cat. But the leopard is a skilled hunter. It wants to kill the anaconda, then drag it up into a tree away from other hungry predators.

The fight starts. The leopard isn't afraid to approach the snake. The leopard starts nipping and annoying the anaconda's tail end. Bite! Run! Bite! Dodge!

Whenever the snake gets close, the leopard dashes away. It moves closer to the snake's midsection. The leopard has a strong jaw. Bite! Crunch! Shift away! Bite! Bite again! Run!

LEOPARD WINS!

The snake is losing blood. It no longer has the energy to encircle the leopard and try to win. The leopard goes in for the kill. It bites the anaconda in the head. The leopard is heading to the finals. It sees the gorilla nearby!

132

The leopard leaps on top of the gorilla. The gorilla uses its muscular arms to bat the leopard away. The leopard bites at the gorilla, but the gorilla grabs the smaller animal by the neck. The leopard retreats. They fight back and forth.

Four legs versus two legs and two arms. Claws versus nails. Spots versus no spots. Cat versus ape. This is the fight we have been waiting for!

The gorilla gets tired of fighting. But it is smart. It sees a big log and picks it up. As the leopard charges, the gorilla swings the log and smacks the leopard, breaking some bones. The big cat is in trouble.

Now the gorilla picks up a heavy rock and drops it on the wounded leopard's head. The fight is over. The gorilla wins. The gorilla may have won, but it hopes it never has to fight a giant cat again.

GORILLA WINS!

This is one way the competition might have ended. Write your own ending or think of a new version of an Ultimate Rumble book.

WHO WOULD WIN?

ULTIMATE SHARK RUMBLE

16-SHARK BRACKET

round 1

basking shark
bull shark
mako shark
saw shark
seven-gilled shark
hammerhead shark
goblin shark
tiger shark
great white shark
lemon shark
whale shark
blacktip shark
thresher shark
leopard shark
megamouth shark
Greenland shark

round 2

winner
winner
winner
winner
winner
winner
winner
winner

round 3

winner
winner
winner
winner

championship

winner
winner

Ultimate Shark Rumble champion

What would happen if 16 sharks were invited to a contest? What if there was a bracketed fight? Who would win? If a shark loses a round, it is out of the competition.

NAME FACT
The basking shark got its name from basking in, or lying in, the sun.

The basking shark is a filter feeder. It swims with its mouth open near the surface of the ocean. Don't be afraid. It has teeny, tiny teeth.

ROUND 1 BASKING SHARK VS. BULL SHARK MATCH 1

The bull shark is a man-eating shark. It moves in shallow water, where some people swim. It also swims up rivers and sometimes into lakes. The bull shark *does* attack people. Beware!

STRANGE FACT
Bull sharks live well in captivity.

No big teeth? Only a filter-feeder jaw? The basking shark does not stand a chance. The bull shark's strong jaw and sharp teeth bite chunks out of the basking shark. Good-bye, basking shark!

TRUE STORY
A bull shark that swam up a river in Africa got eaten by a crocodile.

BULL SHARK WINS!

The shortfin mako shark is the fastest shark in the ocean. It can swim up to 45 miles per hour. Makos are often called the "cheetahs of the sea" or "falcons of the ocean." It is nice to be able to outswim your enemies.

ROUND 1 — MAKO SHARK VS. SAW SHARK — MATCH 2

The saw shark has teeth along its nose. It is an easy shark to identify. It uses its nose to slash at a school of fish. How would you like to have teeth on your nose?

The saw shark is scary looking, but it is no match for a mako. The lightning-fast mako swims right at the saw shark and bites its tail off. The saw shark is wounded and cannot swim.

MAKO SHARK WINS!

Mammals have lungs. Fish have gills. Almost all sharks have five gill slits on each side of their heads. True to its name, the seven-gilled shark has seven gills.

> **FACT**
> *Sharks do not have bones. Their skeletons are made of cartilage, the same kind of material in your nose.*

SEVEN-GILLED SHARK VS. HAMMERHEAD SHARK

Its head doesn't look like a hammer to me. It looks more like an airplane wing. When people see that shape, they know exactly what kind of shark it is.

> **HAMMERHEAD FACT**
> *Its eyes are positioned to have excellent vision.*

> **FACT**
> *One kind of hammerhead shark is known as a bonnethead.*

The hammerhead has excellent vision and can see backward. It is watching the seven-gilled shark's every move. When the seven-gilled shark makes a wrong turn, the bigger hammerhead attacks. One bite! Two bites! Good-bye, seven-gilled shark.

FACT
There is also a rare six-gilled shark.

HAMMERHEAD WINS!

The deep-water goblin shark has a scary-looking "double" face. This shark species has been on Earth for more than 100 million years. Its ancestors probably had fights with plesiosaurs and dinosaurs.

RARE FACT
Few goblin sharks have ever been caught.

FOSSIL FACT
A plesiosaur is an extinct ocean reptile.

GOBLIN SHARK VS. TIGER SHARK

MATCH 4

Meet the tiger shark. It has the perfect name. Surfers and swimmers beware! The tiger shark is known for attacking humans. It has teeth capable of biting tough sea-turtle shells.

SPECIES FACT
A sand tiger shark is a different species than a tiger shark.

This fight is a matchup between an ancient, ugly shark and a sleek, beautifully designed fighting machine. The tiger shark has a larger tail and bigger fins, and it can swim faster and turn better than the goblin shark. The fight does not take long.

SPIRIT FACT
Some Native Hawaiians believe that tiger sharks are the spirits of their ancestors.

TIGER SHARK WINS!

FREE-RIDE FACT
Shark suckers are fish that attach themselves to sharks. They are also called remoras.

The great white shark is one of the most famous sharks in the world. It has a huge, strong jaw with triangle-shaped, serrated teeth. It gets blamed for the most attacks on humans around the world.

FIN FACTS
Sharks have pectoral fins, dorsal fins, pelvic fins, anal fins, and caudal fins.

DORSAL FINS

CAUDAL FIN

ANAL FIN

PELVIC FINS

PECTORAL FINS

ROUND **1**

GREAT WHITE SHARK VS. LEMON SHARK

MATCH **5**

This shark has a light yellow color. Wow—it is different. It has two dorsal fins.

COLOR FACT
Not all sharks are gray.

The lemon shark puts up a good fight, but the great white shark is too big, too strong, and too ferocious for the lemon shark. The great white shark swims right at the lemon shark and uses its powerful jaw to bite the lemon shark. The big bite is fatal.

GREAT WHITE SHARK WINS!

The whale shark is the largest and longest fish in the ocean. It grows up to 40 feet long and weighs up to 20 tons. It has tiny teeth and is a filter feeder. The whale shark swims with its huge mouth open. It strains, or catches, small sea creatures such as krill and copepods. Strange but true: The biggest fish eats the tiniest creatures.

FACT
The whale shark is not a whale.
Like all sharks, it is a fish.

MOUTH FACT
A whale shark's mouth is up to five feet
wide. It looks like a giant vacuum cleaner.

ROUND 1 WHALE SHARK VS. BLACKTIP SHARK MATCH 6

The blacktip shark got its name from the black tip on its dorsal fin. Blacktip sharks are aggressive. They move toward human swimmers.

It's just not fair—an aggressive shark against a filter feeder. The blacktip shark is not intimidated by the size of the whale shark. It swims and bites at the whale shark. Bites, bites, and more bites. The blacktip shark wounds the bigger whale shark.

The whale shark loses too much blood. It slowly sinks. It will be a giant meal for hundreds of other fish.

FACT
A whale shark is the largest vertebrate animal on Earth that is not a mammal.

DEFINITION
Vertebrate *means an animal with a spine.*

DEFINITION
A whale fall is when a whale dies and sinks to the deep bottom of the ocean. There, its skeleton becomes a home and dinner for other sea creatures.

BLACKTIP SHARK WINS!

The thresher shark has a long tail. Its tail is more than half the length of its body. The tail allows it to swim, turn, and stop faster. It hunts using its tail to whip at schools of fish.

FACT
Common thresher sharks are also called fox sharks.

THRESHER SHARK VS. LEOPARD SHARK

The leopard shark is a small shark that has leopard-like spots. It grows to only about four feet long.

SMALL FACT
The dwarf lantern shark is the smallest shark in the ocean. It is only about eight inches long.

COOLEST NAME
The tiny cookiecutter shark cuts little cookie-shaped chunks out of other fish, dolphins, and whales.

The thresher shark circles the leopard shark to check it out. There is a huge size difference between this pair. The thresher shark uses its big tail to whip and stun the leopard shark. Its unusual tail is like a secret weapon.

LANGUAGE FACT
In Spanish, a shark is called el tiburón.

THRESHER SHARK WINS!

The megamouth is a big, long shark with a wide mouth. This rare deep-water shark was discovered in 1976. Don't be scared. Big mouth. Big lips. No big deal! This shark is also a filter feeder.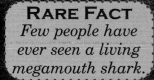

RARE FACT
Few people have ever seen a living megamouth shark.

NO CONFUSION
Don't mix up the megamouth with a megalodon, the largest shark that ever lived. The prehistoric megalodon is extinct.

MEGAMOUTH VS. GREENLAND SHARK

Greenland sharks are also called gurry sharks or gray sharks. They live the longest of any shark—between 300 and 500 years. That's a lot of birthday parties. The Greenland shark belongs to a shark species that has been on Earth more than 100 million years.

TRICKY NAME
Gurry are the parts left over after you fillet, or debone, a fish. Gurry is often used for crab and lobster bait.

The megamouth usually eats tiny fish and krill—it wouldn't know how to attack the Greenland shark. The Greenland shark swims toward the megamouth. The hungry Greenland shark attacks the megamouth.

BUMP FACT
Some sharks bump first to try to figure out what a creature or object is made of.

FACT
Greenland sharks have been found swimming one mile below the ocean's surface.

The megamouth has lots of teeth but they are small and useless in a fight like this. The Greenland shark chews up the megamouth.

GREENLAND SHARK WINS!

We're at the end of the first round. Only eight sharks are left in the competition.

The bull shark fought a filter feeder to get into round 2. Now it faces speed and sharp teeth. This is a challenge. Who will win? Who will get into the SHARK FINAL FOUR?

BULL SHARK VS. MAKO SHARK

ROUND 2

MATCH 1

The mako is so fast that the bull shark has trouble finding it. The bull shark has trouble chasing its opponent.

ATTACK FACTS
Some sharks attack from below. Other sharks attack from above.

Speed is a great weapon, but eventually the mako has to confront the bull shark. The bull shark is too strong and too nasty for the mako. The bull shark overpowers the mako. The bull shark has a stronger jaw!

BULL SHARK WINS!

Some people thought the hammerhead might end up in the championship match against the tiger shark, but they must meet in the second round.

ROUND 2
HAMMERHEAD SHARK VS. TIGER SHARK
MATCH 2

TAG-ALONG FACT
Pilot fish get protection and leftover food by following sharks as they swim.

The hammerhead has a smaller mouth than the tiger shark. The tiger shark glides to the side and bites off one of the hammerhead's eyes. The hammerhead is in trouble. The tiger shark then bites it in the back.

TIGER SHARK WINS!

Could the great white shark eat every other shark in this book? Too bad the extinct megalodon isn't around to swallow the great white shark with one bite. The great white shark starts swimming toward the blacktip shark.

TAIL FACT
Sea mammals have horizontal tails. Almost all sharks have vertical tails.

GREAT WHITE SHARK VS. BLACKTIP SHARK

The blacktip shark sees the great white shark and realizes this is a serious contest. There is no place to hide.

PACK FACT
Blacktip sharks are often found in large packs, or groups.

The great white shark attacks. It hides its eyes as it opens its huge jaw and wounds the blacktip shark. The aggressive blacktip shark wants to escape but it's too late. It becomes lunch.

GREAT WHITE SHARK WINS!

The thresher shark, with its fancy tail and tricky turns, tries to intimidate the Greenland shark. Its strategy does not work.

ROUND 2
THRESHER SHARK VS. GREENLAND SHARK
MATCH 4

The Greenland shark is bigger and not scared. It is ready to show off its strong jaw.

DENTAL FACT
A shark loses thousands of teeth during its lifetime. It grows new ones to replace them. Humans only have 32 adult teeth.

When the thresher shark swims near, the Greenland shark bites a chunk out of the thresher shark.

The thresher shark is overcome by the Greenland shark's strength. Don't mess with an old pro!

GREENLAND SHARK WINS!

That's it! The SHARK FINAL FOUR is set. Bull shark, tiger shark, great white shark, and Greenland shark! All the filter feeders are gone.

There are only four competitors left. Should we call it ROUND 3, FIGHT 1? Or the Semifinals? Oh, right! It's the

SHARK FINAL FOUR

This is a fight of almost equals. Both are ferocious sharks. Each is considered a "man-eater." The bull shark and tiger shark are often in the news.

ROUND **3**

BULL SHARK VS. TIGER SHARK

MATCH **1**

The bull shark approaches the tiger shark. The tiger shark goes after the bull shark. The tiger shark is longer and heavier. The bull shark is broader.

This is a serious fight. Someone is going to get hurt. The tiger shark overpowers the bull shark. *Crunch!*

The bull shark slowly sinks.

TIGER SHARK WINS!

The great white shark waits for the Greenland shark to swim toward the surface. They are about the same size. The great white shark is a faster swimmer. Its teeth are bigger and sharper.

ROUND 3 GREAT WHITE SHARK VS. GREENLAND SHARK MATCH 2

The Greenland shark is not as agile, or able to move as quickly, as the great white. The great white shark is more intelligent. What is the great white's strategy?

MOVIE FACT
The great white shark starred in four famous movies: Jaws, Jaws 2, Jaws 3-D, *and* Jaws: The Revenge.

At full speed the great white shark attacks from below. *Crunch!* It rips the soft underbelly of the Greenland shark. The great white shark knew it did not want its first bite to be against the Greenland shark's tougher topside. Good-bye, Greenland shark!

GREAT WHITE SHARK WINS!

We should have known the movie star great white shark would make it to the finals!

CHAMPIONSHIP MATCH!
TIGER SHARK VS. GREAT WHITE SHARK

Two ferocious sharks battle back and forth. Tiger shark versus great white shark! A blunt head against a pointy head. Eyes on the side versus eyes up front. A square jaw confronts an oval jaw.

The great white shark tries to attack from below. The tiger shark stays close to the bottom. As the great white swims by, the tiger shark, with its longer tail, makes a quick turn and bites into the great white. The great white shark is bleeding.

The tiger shark is skinnier than the wide great white. In most fights, a great white shark would win, but today is different. In this battle, the tiger shark is a better warrior.

TIGER SHARK WINS!

This is one way the competition might have ended. Write your own ending or think of a new version of an Ultimate Rumble book.

REWRITE THE ULTIMATE OCEAN RUMBLE BRACKET!

In our version, the saltwater crocodile won the tournament. Rewrite the bracket so that each animal is facing someone different. Who would win in your version?

16-CREATURE BRACKET

round 1

round 2

round 3

championship

Blue-ringed octopus
Killer whale

Man o'war
Stonefish

Great white shark
Giant manta ray

Walrus
Narwhal

Sand tiger shark
Sea snake

Leatherback turtle
Giant Squid

Polar bear
Torpedo fish

Saltwater crocodile
Sailfish

Ultimate Ocean Rumble champion

REWRITE THE ULTIMATE BUG RUMBLE BRACKET!

In our version, the hornet won the tournament. Rewrite the bracket so that each animal is facing someone different. Who would win in your version?

16-CREATURE BRACKET

round 1

round 2

round 3

championship

Butterfly
Dragonfly

Assassin bug
Killer bee

Tarantula
Black widow spider

Centipede
Cockroach

Hornet
Stinkbug

Daddy longlegs
Cicada

Woolly bear
Tiger beetle

Scorpion
Praying mantis

Ultimate
Bug
Rumble
champion

REWRITE THE ULTIMATE DINOSAUR RUMBLE BRACKET!

In our version, the Spinosaurus won the tournament. Rewrite the bracket so that each animal is facing someone different. Who would win in your version?

16-CREATURE BRACKET

round 1
round 2
round 3
championship

Apatosaurus
Spinosaurus
Tyrannosaurus Rex
Kentrosaurus
Ankylosaurus
Utahraptor
Torosaurus
Supersaurus
Gigantosaurus
Tyrannotitan
Styracosaurus
Allosaurus
Megalosaurus
Yangchuanosaurus
Micropachycephalosaurus
Stegosaurus

Ultimate
Dinosaur
Rumble
champion

REWRITE THE ULTIMATE JUNGLE RUMBLE BRACKET!

In our version, the gorilla won the tournament. Rewrite the bracket so that each animal is facing someone different. Who would win in your version?

16-CREATURE BRACKET

round 1
round 2
round 3
championship

Monitor lizard
Black mamba
Capybara
Red panda
Mandrill
Okapi
Sun bear
Hyena
Gorilla
Poison dart frog
Peacock
Warthog
Green anaconda
Leopard
Anteater
Bongo

Ultimate
Jungle
Rumble
champion

REWRITE THE ULTIMATE SHARK RUMBLE BRACKET!

In our version, the tiger shark won the tournament. Rewrite the bracket so that each animal is facing someone different. Who would win in your version?

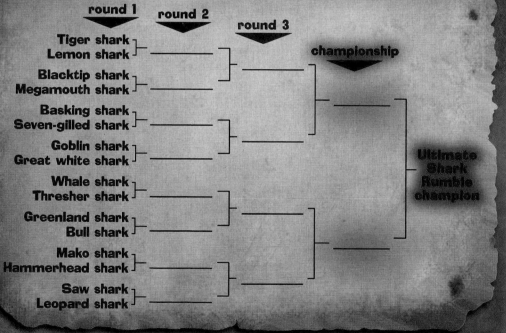

16-CREATURE BRACKET

round 1

round 2

round 3

championship

Tiger shark
Lemon shark

Blacktip shark
Megamouth shark

Basking shark
Seven-gilled shark

Goblin shark
Great white shark

Whale shark
Thresher shark

Greenland shark
Bull shark

Mako shark
Hammerhead shark

Saw shark
Leopard shark

Ultimate Shark Rumble champion

EXTREME
ANIMAL
RUMBLE